I0136157

New Year's Resolutions, Goals, Dreams and Aspirations

Suzanne J. Price

www.suzanneprice.com

www.newyearresolutions.info

SJP

Coaching &

Consulting

Coaching To Inspire, Motivate, Challenge & Bring About Positive Change

New Year Resolutions

Goals, Dreams and

Aspirations

Copyright © 2011 by Suzanne J. Price

Canadian Intellectual Property Certificate of
Registration 2011

Published by Suzanne J. Price

Book cover designed by Debbie Deem

All rights reserved. No part of this book may be used or
reproduced in any manner whatsoever without prior
written consent of the author.

ISBN 978-0-9812862-1-1

Dedicated To You

This book is dedicated to anyone who has a dream, who dares to set goals, or who aspires to live a happier, healthier life. No matter who you are, where you've been or what burdens you carry with you. You, need to believe in yourself and follow your heart, as everyone deserves to live a life filled with passion and purpose.

This book is especially dedicated to my Grandmother Monica and my Nephew Neil and to everyone who I've crossed paths with in my life, and have bestowed upon me fond memories that will last a lifetime.

Thank You!

Title Page

New Year's Resolutions   Page 11

Why Clearly Defined Goals & Positive Thinking
Don't Necessarily Work   Page 19

Finding Clarity In Your Life and Creating Crystal
Clear Goals   Page25

Ranking Your Goals For Importance and

Priority   Page 39

How To Make Sure That The Negative Anchors
Which May Have Been Created By Move Away
From or Recurring Goals Do Not Sabotage Your
Future Success   Page 45

A Word About Positive Thinking And The Law Of
Attraction   Page51

There Is No Secret To It, You Have To Take
Action If You Want To Succeed Page 59

Pick A Goal And Create Your Vision   Page61

Title Page

Connecting With And Attaching Yourself To Your Goal   Page 69

Motivational Strategies   Page 77

Recognizing And Dealing With Obstacles, Objections and Conflicting Beliefs   Page 89

Maintaining Balance In Your Life While Achieving Your Goals, Dreams, Aspirations and New Year's Resolutions. Page 99

Why Work With A Coach?   Page 103

New Year Resolution Planner   Page 109

S.M.A.R.T. Goal Planner   Page 123

A Note From Suzanne on Passion, Purpose & The Importance Of Goals.

2012 A Time For Change

There has been a lot of talk about 2012. With all of the fears about the world coming to an end and the rumours about New Beginnings, nobody really knows what to expect. So maybe, if we chose to believe that the world will end as we know it, and collectively we take action to create a better world to live in, then surely together we can look forward to many new things to come.

In an effort to make our world a better place we can all take part in our own special way and do whatever feels right for us.

My personal mission is that first, I want to help people find passion and purpose in their life so that they can live their life to the fullest. This I will do through writing and teaching workshops and webinars, as well as personal coaching.

And secondly, the thing that I feel most passionate about is that I want to help people connect, or reconnect with each other, whichever the case may be. I'd like to help people build and experience real, genuine, deeper and more meaningful relationships throughout their lives. I believe that this connection will contribute to making this planet a happier, safer and more united place to live. And hope to achieve this through my books, coaching, teaching and writing.

What's your mission?

Please join this movement, 2012 A Time For Change, by signing up on www.newyearresolutions.info where you can share your ideas. Each week I will post a new idea, or positive attitude towards change, and hope to introduce a thought provoking topic. I'd love to hear your ideas so please share them online.

While on the site you will also be able to create your own profile page and post and share your own New Year Resolutions. You will also have the option to connect with new people and support each other to succeed.

Throughout the year you will also find new tips, tools, videos and great ideas on making positive change and succeeding with your goals. And I will post any upcoming workshops, webinars or events geared towards living life with passion and purpose

This site and app will be launched in 2012

New Year's Resolutions

- ❖ Get into shape
- ❖ Meet the love of my life
- ❖ Become a happier person
- ❖ Have more balance in my life
- ❖ Spend more time with family & friends
- ❖ Take dance lessons
- ❖ Learn to speak Spanish
- ❖ Take up a new hobby
- ❖ Start having more of a social life
- ❖ Take a cooking class
- ❖ Hire a personal success coach
- ❖ SUCCEED AT FULFILLING MY DAMN NEW YEAR'S RESOLUTIONS

It's that time of year again, the New Year! It's the time of year which gives us the opportunity to wipe the slate clean. It's when we get to put all of our past failed attempts behind us so that we can have a fresh start and enter the New Year determined to make this be the year that counts.

This will be the year that success and dreams are made of, and the year that could potentially change your life. It's time to reinvent yourself, and show the world what you are made of, and to make that promise to yourself to live your life to the fullest.

Nothing is going to get in your way. Nothing, that is except for life itself! And of course those nagging thoughts and feelings of self doubt which constantly remind you of the goals, dreams, aspirations and New Year resolutions you've made in the past, but you never followed through. And how weeks, months or even years down the road you looked back only to realize that you had let yourself down. And, well let's just tell it as it is... YOU FAILED!

But that is all in the past. And even though you may feel as though those past failed attempts have set precedence for future success, this definitely does not have to be the case. In fact, if you really do want to start fulfilling your goals and you are willing to put in the time and effort, you can succeed at anything.

It can take a lot to achieve a goal, and in particular a New Year Resolution, but it is well worth the effort.

And the added rewards and benefits which you could gain along the way may have the potential to go way beyond the success of achieving any goal. So if you are up for the challenge and you are willing to commit to the process, you may discover that achieving your goals or succeeding with your New Year Resolutions could literally change your life.

When you commit to a goal and you follow through for yourself not only will you reap the rewards of satisfaction, fulfillment and pride, but you will also develop a set of life skills that you will be able to apply to any area of your life. And with these skills you will eventually be able to achieve anything that your heart desires.

Goal setting and following through on your New Year Resolutions can be an incredible way for adults and children alike to learn some invaluable life skills.

Some of these skills may include fulfilling personal commitments, time management, organizational skills, goal setting, planning, creative thinking, problem solving, brain storming, flexibility, self discipline, personal awareness, practicing determination, dedication, strategizing, creativity, creating and maintain balance in life, self motivation and inspiration. All of which contribute to building confidence in your abilities to succeed as well as in yourself.

The process of committing to and actually achieving your goals and New Year Resolutions can be such an empowering experience. And developing these positive and powerful goal achievement habits, and building blocks for success could make the difference of whether or not you will go on in life to fulfill your dreams, become the person you aspire to be, or ultimately live the life you want to live. So if you are ready, willing and able to make this commitment to yourself, then I would love to help. And that is exactly what inspired me to write this book, New Year's Resolutions, Goals, Dreams & Aspirations.

I designed and wrote this goals achievement program with the purpose of helping you to succeed at achieving any of your goals, dreams, aspirations and New Year's Resolutions. It is a book which is not just about setting goals, but it is about achieving them too. And is unique not only in the way that it will really help you understand what it takes to set and achieve great goals, but more importantly it will also help you become aware of what may prevent you from achieving them too.

Throughout this book you will have the opportunity to experience and work with some exercises based on NLP, mind/body therapies and coaching practices which I use in my life every day, and which are invaluable tools when it comes to achieving your goals.

I have also included some exercises which will help you to understand why achieving your goals may have been such a challenge in the past. And which will help you to uncover some of the obstacles and hurdles which if left unchecked, could continue to sabotage you in the future. Then with your new awareness, and with the help of some very powerful tools you will be able to take action to eliminate these obstacles and hurdles so that they will be less likely to interfere with your success in the future.

As you work through this book you will also be able to uncover some of the little details which are so often over looked when attempting to achieve your goals. This process is paramount especially as it is often these details which have the power to sabotage and prevent you from experiencing success.

I have also included an exercise to help you create crystal clear move towards goals as well as some tools which will allow you to detach any negative thoughts or feeling which may have been generated by, and become attached to, any past, present or future goals that you have not been able to experience any success with yet.

By the end of the book you be able to recognize the various motivational strategies that we all unconsciously live by every day, and which have the power to either help or hinder our achievements. And you will become very aware of which motivational styles and strategies you usually use in *your* own life. I will also show you how to turn any negative influences into positive empowering resources that will help turn your goals into a reality.

By the time you have finished the program you will probably have uncovered some of the little saboteurs that may have prevented you from succeeding in the past. And as you work through the exercises you may eliminate them so that they will be less likely to prevent you from succeeding in the future.

And by the time you have finished this book not only will you have a whole new set of skills to take and apply to any area of your life, but you will also have a new understanding of just how important it is to follow through with, and achieve your goals. And you will realize how by creating and applying these powerful and positive goal achievement habits you will eventually be able to achieve anything that you want in life. You will be able to become anything you want to be, and you will be able to live the life you dream of.

In a nutshell, I would like to share with you the secrets of turning every one of your goals, dreams, aspirations and New Year's Resolutions into a reality.

If you are willing to make the commitment to yourself and to follow each and every one of the exercises in this book, and put them into practice, you will ultimately have the opportunity to experience some of your greatest successes yet.

This year my dear friends, is going to be different! It is time to make this be the year that you start to achieve all of your goals, dreams and aspiration. And by starting with your New Year Resolutions you will eventually be able to succeed at achieving anything your heart desires. Here's to you and all of your successes.

Good luck and Happy New Year!

Suzanne

Why Clearly Defined Goals & Positive Thinking

Don't Necessarily Work

The truth is that if you have not succeeded at achieving your goals, dreams or past New Year's resolutions, it is not your fault. For too long now, we have been led to believe that if we have a plan, a set of clearly defined goals and we simply think positively that we should be able to achieve anything. Although all three aspects are very important to achieving success, when it comes to fulfilling your goals and dreams, there is much more at play than what meets the eye.

I'm talking about all of those hidden little factors, such as negative or limiting beliefs which we are often not even aware of having, motivational strategies, and self sabotaging behaviours that we live with on a daily basis. These saboteurs run like internal programs which may be so ingrained it is as if they are concealed in our subconscious mind. And, perhaps without even realizing it, it is often these forces at play that prevent us from experiencing success in any area of our lives.

These sabotaging beliefs and behaviours, or habits as it were can create an internal turmoil which will inhibit us from following through and succeeding in future attempts. However they are often so ingrained that they are difficult for us to detect on our own. If this is the case, we may need the help of a coach to assist us to bring them into our conscious awareness, as becoming aware of these saboteurs is one of the first things that needs to happen in order for us to move forward.

Every time we fail to follow through on our commitments to ourselves, we are letting ourselves down and feeding the habit of self-sabotage. This habit may leave us feeling disappointed, defeated and even doomed, and we may even end up developing an underlying belief that we are not worth our own efforts. This behaviour will likely start to erode away at our self esteem, but following through may not be as easy as it sounds.

Whenever we are not achieving what we want, whether it is to lose weight, find the perfect job, or become more confident and outgoing so that we can meet and attract our ideal mate, there is usually at least one of the following forces at play. We are either sabotaging ourselves with our own self limiting beliefs, we are using ineffective motivational strategies, or there is some sort of fear present.

When we want change we first need to identify exactly what we want. We can do this by shaking everything up and chipping away at all the crud in our minds so that we can get a clear view of what our goals and desires really look like. In order to make our goals crystal clear we will also need to figure out if they are related to a thought, a feeling or an emotion, a behaviour, or if they require us to either acquire or dispose of some*thing*.

For some people their goal may be that they want to experience life differently, saying something like "I want to be happy" or "I don't want to be such an angry person anymore". However until they identify the thoughts and behaviours that prevent them from being happy, or cause them to fly off the handle, they may find it impossible to experience that desired state.

Beliefs can also get in the way causing us to feel hopeless and helpless whenever we feel stuck. You have to believe that it is both possible to achieve your goal and that *you* are capable of achieving it, or at least willing to seek the help and knowledge to do so.

If you think that a goal is impossible to achieve, then it will be, and if you think that you personally are not capable of achieving it, you won't. In either event it is unlikely that you will take the necessary steps to achieve your success. The good thing about beliefs is that with the right awareness and an open mind we can change them.

Motivational strategies are also a huge part of achieving our goals. One of the motivational strategies we all use unconsciously is that we typically move towards what we want, or we move away from what we don't want. Very often we focus on what we don't want and not on what we do. By focussing on what we don't want two things happen. First the brain doesn't know the difference between what is positive or what is negative, so consequently whatever you think about is exactly what you are going to get.

Secondly, if we think about what we don't want in hopes of getting away from it, our motivation is to move away from it as opposed to moving towards or being drawn towards what we actually do want. The problem is that when we move away from something, we tend to move only just far enough away from it to avoid the pain that it causes us, and not far enough in the right direction to get what we want instead.

And if all this isn't enough to stop us from achieving our goals, there is sometimes an unconscious self sabotaging phenomenon that we need to shift before we can abolish any limiting beliefs or fears which stop us from moving forward. It's no wonder that so many people have such a hard time achieving their goals, dreams and greatest desires, never mind sticking to their New Year's Resolutions.

To successfully achieve any goal you need to enrol in a process of awareness, flexibility, creativity, action and determination just to name a few, but it is well worth the effort. Just thinking positively rarely works because first of all we have to put all of the pieces into action, and secondly, if we don't actually believe a goal to be attainable it will probably just cause us more stress and frustration.

The good news is that anything is possible, and my goal with this book is to help you uncover all of the nitty, gritty little details that often get in the way of your success. And I'd like to offer you some tools which will help you to move forward on a path to success so that you can achieve any of your goals, and stick with your New Year's Resolutions.

As a coach I can also help you overcome your fears, identify your self-sabotaging behaviours and challenge you to identify all of the aspects of your life which are unsatisfactory. I can also help you to develop crystal clear goals and assist you to identify and utilize your best personal motivational strategies. I can inspire, motivate and challenge you to succeed in all of your personal, professional and emotional goals, while encouraging you to create more balance in your life.

With the right awareness and tools you will soon be able to achieve any goals, dreams, aspirations and New Year's Resolutions which may have previously seemed unattainable.

Finding Clarity In Your Life and Creating Crystal Clear Goals

S.M.A.R.T. Goals

The chances are that if you have done any research at all on how to achieve your goals, you will by now at least be aware of SMART goals. SMART standing for:

S = Specific or Stated in the positive

M = Measurable

A = Achievable, Attainable, Actionable

R = Realistic

T = Timely or Tangible

SMART is a very good guideline for setting goals, however to achieve them takes a lot more than simply setting them. For instance we need to be able to connect with and identify with our goals, and we need to believe that we are capable of achieving them. And in order to succeed we also need to develop and exercise skills that we don't often even think about. You will be utilizing these skills as you work through the exercises in this book.

The Power Of Knowing Exactly What You Want

Most people have goals, but they are often unaware of how to go about achieving them. This may be because they either do not know *exactly* what it is that they want to achieve, why they want to achieve them, or what it is going to take to turn their goals into a reality.

Some people have great goals, or at least a very clear vision. And yet others have no idea what they want at all.

Many of us are simply aware that we want to experience some sort of change in our life, however we do not necessarily know what it is that we would like, or need to change. And often the only awareness we have of this need for change comes from within, and may present itself in the form of an uneasy feeling such as loneliness, restlessness, anger, resentment, sadness or despair.

If we are lucky these feelings may bring about a vague awareness of what we think we might want instead of our current unwanted situation. But in reality these feelings can create turmoil and will cause most people to feel well and truly stuck.

The good news is that no matter how stuck we feel, or think we are, as long as we commit to being brutally honest with ourselves we can develop an awareness which will set us free. And this may not be as difficult as it sounds.

The key to unlocking this turmoil and setting ourselves free is to find clarity in our lives, and to become extremely clear about exactly what it is that we truly do want. When we become aware of what we want we can then create our goals, but it is often when trying to find this awareness that so many people get stumped.

With this in mind then it should only make sense that the first thing that we need to do in order to experience any sort of change or success is to become aware of what we really want. This is an extremely important piece of the puzzle as it will help to build a strong foundation for success.

The following exercises will help you to shake up all of that crud in your mind which may have been causing you confusion and hindering your progress in the past. With this clarity you will then be able to create crystal clear goals.

To Find Clarity In Your Life & Create Crystal Clear Goals You May Need To First Become Aware Of , And Acknowledge The Things In Your Life That Are Not Serving You Well

Sometimes when we are feeling stuck and are not sure what we want, or we just don't know how to go about getting it, it is best to start by becoming aware of, and acknowledging all the things in our life where we would like to experience change. This is usually the best place to start especially as when we are in such a place of confusion, we are usually more aware of what is bothering us, or of what we do not want, than what we do want anyway.

The first step to finding clarity in your life is to list the things that you know that you are not happy with, or the areas of your life that you would like to experience change. This will help you define specific goals. However if you already have some specific goals or New Year Resolutions then you may chose to do these exercises around them, in order to make sure that they are positive, move towards goals.

Following is a list of examples of some of the most common areas where people want to experience change in their life, and how they often *state* them. These issues often come up when people are making New Year Resolutions.

I'm sick and tired of being broke

I hate my job

I'm lonely being single

I'm stuck in a dead end job

I hate driving an old car

I really should quit smoking

I'm always broke

I'm always late

I'm so disorganized

I'm always so stressed out

I hate throwing away money on rent

I never have any fun

I always end up in bad relationships

My life is doomed

I hate being overweight

I'm so out of shape

I don't like the way I look

I don't know what I want to do with my life

I'm useless at doing... (Whatever that may be for you personally)

I'm fed up with living on junk food

I never have anyone to do things with

I've given up on meeting Mr. Right

The only social life I have is with my computer

If I don't find a wife soon I probably never will

When goals are thought of, and stated in the negative such as these are, we call them Move Away From Goals. They are goals in the manner that we are aware of wanting to change something, but at the same time because they are stated in the negative they can keep us stuck.

Often when we are only aware of our move away from goals we can feel really trapped. And when this happens our vision can become clouded, making it easy to become consumed by the negative thoughts and feelings surrounding our goal. When in this state it would be easy to become overwhelmed, making it difficult for us to imagine how there could be any other way of being, or that we do in fact have options to change our experience.

Many people go through life in this stuck state, and this can cause them to feel as though there is no way out. If these feelings persist they may even end up giving up hope that they will ever be able to achieve anything in life. And they may ultimately end up feeling defeated or even doomed.

The unfortunate thing about living with these negative thoughts and feelings is that unless we recognize them, and identify what options we have available to change our experience around them, we may think that the only way we will get to experience change is to eliminate this particular part of our life. And this could be a huge mistake.

The simplest and easiest solution to get out of such a predicament is to turn our negative move away from goals into positive move towards goals instead. This is a process that can be easily done with the following exercise.

List Of Move Away From Goals

It is now time to create your list of Move Away From Goals.

How To Turn Our Negative Thoughts, Feelings, Behaviours And Statements Into Crystal Clear Move Towards Goals

Now that we are aware of how our Move Away From Goals can keep us stuck, we are going to start to create some crystal clear, Move Towards Goals.

To do so we are going to replace each one of our Move Away From Goals or negative statements with a positive Move Towards Goal. Going back to your original list of Move Away From Goals, look at each item that you no longer want, then on the page labelled, Move Towards Goals, write down what you want instead. You are looking for the positive solution or the ultimate goal. You do not have to be too specific at this point.

Here are some examples of positive statements or move towards goals which would replace your move away from goals.

Move Away From Goals	Move Towards Goals
I'm sick and tired of being broke	I want to make more money
I hate my job	I am going to find a job I love
I'm lonely being single	I'm ready to meet someone special
I'm stuck in a dead end job	I can change my job
I hate driving an old car	I'm going to buy a new car
I really should quit smoking	I've made a decision to quit smoking
I'm always broke	I am going to improve my financial situation
I'm always late	I am going start being punctual
I'm so disorganized	It is time to organize my life
I'm always so stressed out	I will practice stress management techniques
I hate throwing away money on rent	I want to buy my own home
I never have any fun	I'm ready to have more fun
I always end up in bad relationships	I will only date men/women who will treat me well
My life is doomed	I am going to take control of my destiny
I hate being overweight	I'm going to work with a weight loss coach
I'm so out of shape	I am joining the gym and a

	running club
I don't like the way I look	I'm going to get a makeover
I'm useless at doing...	I can learn anything I set my mind too
I'm fed up with living on junk food	I'm going to change my diet
I never have anyone to do things with	I want to make some new friends
I've given up on meeting Mr. Right	I am going to hire a relationship coach
The only social life I have is with my computer	I am going to join some social groups
If I don't find a wife soon	I want to meet that one special woman who I will want to spend the rest of my life with

List Of Move Towards Goals

It is now time to create your list of positively stated goals. To do so start by looking at each one of your Move Away From Goals, and then think about what you want instead of that present unwanted experience. Now create a list of what you actually want instead.

Move Towards Goals

Going back to the S in SMART goals, you have now created a set of goals which are Stated In The Positive. However, they are probably not yet quite specific enough to inspire or motivate you to succeed. But you will have very Specific Goals by the time you have finished the next few chapters, and are ready to take action.

If you have any other goals, dreams, aspirations or New Year's Resolutions that come to mind, and they are already stated in the positive, you can add them to this list.

Ranking Your Goals For Importance and Priority

Our attitudes and behaviours towards our goals and commitments can have a huge impact on every area of our lives. Not only can achieving a goal set you on a new path in life which in turn could literally have the power to be a life altering experience. But by simply following through and achieving a goal, this could also have a very positive impact on your self esteem, your confidence and your mental and emotional health.

Every time we achieve one of our goals we fulfill a promise to ourselves that we will make good on our own personal commitments. This can be an extremely empowering experience as it can instil in us the belief that we have the power to achieve our goals as well as to succeed in life. And, that we can trust ourselves to do whatever it takes to succeed.

The success of achieving a goal will also help us to become confident in knowing that we can succeed again, and will inspire us to continue to develop and practice good habits around achieving our own personal success. This will also require us to use our skills of self motivation, determination, creativity and inspiration.

However, if we develop the habit of not following through or we bail on our goals on a regular basis it can have the opposite effect. Then instead of being empowered we may develop some very negative thoughts and feelings around our abilities to achieve our goals. And if we are not careful these thoughts and feelings could turn into some very negative anchors, which could sabotage us in any future attempts at success.

This may apply no matter how big or small a goal is, or whether or not the goal is even important enough for us to want to achieve. So knowing this we should be careful not put our attention on goals that we know we will never follow through with. As not only are we likely to fail with the goal itself, but by not following through we may also be setting ourselves up for failure throughout or lives. Because even if we attempt, or bail on a goal that is not that important to us, it may still have the same negative impact on our self esteem as one which is a high priority would .

Being clear about what we want to achieve will allow us to become very selective about what goals we chose to put our attention on. We need to be careful to only set and commit to goals that we know we are genuinely interested in achieving, that we have the intention to follow through with, and that we have the ability to achieve.

The following exercise will help you identify just how important your goals are to you, and whether or not you will likely do whatever is necessary to bring them to life.

Rate Your Goals

A good way to clarify how important a goal is to you is to rate it on a scale of importance and priority. Do this exercise with any goal you are considering moving forward with as well as with all of your New Year Resolutions.

For this exercise start by selecting one of your goals and then rate it on the following scale. Repeat this exercise with each goal.

On a scale of 1 -10 with 1 meaning that this particular goal is actually nothing more than a good idea, and 10 meaning that it is of high importance and could be a life changing goal, where on the scale of 1-10 would this goal be?

Just An Idea 1-2-3-4-5-6-7-8-9-10 A High Priority Goal

When doing this exercise go with your gut feeling. Do not analyze why you ranked a goal a certain way at this point, nor should you try to rationalize why the goal should be ranked as a higher priority goal, if your gut reaction says otherwise.

If your goal falls between 1 and 5, there is a very good chance that the goal may not be that important to you, or at least not at this point in time. If your goal falls between 6 and 10 then it is definitely a higher priority goal.

Group Your Goals In Order Of Priority

Another way to prioritize your goals is to group them in the following manner.

If you have a goal which falls between 1-3 place it on a list of Good Ideas.

If you rate a goal between 4-7, place it on a list of low to medium priority goals.

If your goal rates between an 8-10, then place it on a list of high priority goals.

Now that you have three separate groups of goals you need to decide what to do with them. My suggestion would be that you take your list of low priority goals, which may actually be just good ideas at this point, and set them aside. And give yourself permission to get back to them if and when you have time at a later date. This will help take some pressure off yourself as you no longer have these particular goals looming in the background.

Then look at your medium and high priority goals and decide which ones you will be most likely to stick with and succeed with at this point in time.

If you are not sure which goals you would like to work on, or if you have a history of letting yourself down and bailing on your goals, then I would first make it a priority to build some confidence around succeeding with your goals. In saying this, I would suggest that you do not select a goal that you do not think you will be able to achieve, or see at least some results with in the near future. Instead choose a goal that you know would be easily attainable. Then stick with it until you have achieved it. This will help you to start building a foundation for success.

Remember success is as much about creating and practicing good goal setting habits as it is about the actual goal itself. Make it a priority to start experiencing some success with your goals. Then before you know it, you will be well on your way to developing the habits which are necessary for achieving success in any area of your life.

If you already have a good track record of achieving your goals, then continue by selecting an important goal that you know will make a difference in your life, and that will help you move towards living the life you want to live.

How To Make Sure That The Negative Anchors Which May Have Been Created By Move Away From or Recurring Goals Do Not Sabotage Your Future Success

Some goals such as a move away from goal which has caused you to feel stuck in the past can carry with it a certain amount of negativity. And if you are not careful that negativity can take on a life of its own. Any opportunity it gets it will invade to create interference by reminding you of all of the reason why you are, or have been stuck.

We call this interference a negative anchor, and if you let them these anchors will crop up to sabotage you every time that you think about attempting to achieve your goals.

Negative anchors can also be created in other ways, and they will attach themselves to other goals, with one such goal being a recurring goal. A recurring goal is one that you have wanted to achieve for some time but have not yet been able to do so. It may or may not be a particularly important goal, but the fact that you would still like to achieve it means that it will probably keep cropping up on your goals, dreams or New Year Resolutions lists over and over again.

The fact that you have not yet been able to achieve your goal may cause you to feel some doubt as to whether or not you will ever follow through with it. And this can create a negative anchor which could cause you to second guess yourself whenever you think about the goal.

However, the thing that is important to know about these anchors is that as long as we are aware of them, we can work with them and in turn prevent them from interfering with our success. And we do this with some exercises which you will find throughout the book.

To find out if a negative anchor is preventing you from achieving a goal, put the goal through this little test.

Select one of your goals and pay attention to how it makes you feel. Notice how when you think about the goal, if it elicits any sort of negativity. Or, if when you think about the fact that you have not yet achieved it, this changes your mood or frame of mind. If it does then there is a very good chance that you have some sort of negative anchor which could sabotage your efforts.

Being aware of the fact that there is some negativity, allows us to take the action necessary to put it to rest. This is an important piece of the process because if we neglect do something about all of these nagging thoughts and feelings which surround any of our goals, dreams, aspirations or New Year's Resolutions, then these anchors can continue to crop up and sabotage us in the future.

The following exercise will help you to detach the negative thoughts and feelings which have probably developed into unconscious negative anchors or obstacles, from the goals themselves. Upon completing this exercise these negative anchors will be less likely to get in the way of your future attempts to achieve your goals.

This is a visual exercise which will help you to put those negative thoughts and feelings behind you, and in turn will help you to change the way you feel towards your goals. This process will allow you to focus on, and put your attention on what you do want to achieve, as you will be less likely to become distracted by doubting yourself because of past failed attempts. This will also help you to create a greater vision of success, and will allow you more flexibility and freedom to move forward.

To do this exercise you will need to be thinking about the negative thoughts and feelings surrounding you move away from, or recurring goals.

As you think about the selected Move Away From Goal, or recurring goal notice how it makes you feel. How do you feel about *not achieving the goal itself*? Also how do you feel about *yourself* with regards to the fact that you have not yet achieved the goal?

If you notice that you have negative thoughts and feeling revolving around this goal or the fact that you have not yet accomplished it, these thoughts will only hinder your progress in the future. As putting any attention on these negative aspects could keep you stuck.

Now that you have acknowledged how these move away from, past failed attempts, or recurring goals make you feel, it is time to come up with a statement which will summarize all of the negative feelings surrounding the goal and the fact that you have not yet achieved it. Only do this exercise on goals which have negative feelings or a negative anchor attached to them.

Next, in your mind, visualize yourself writing the statement on a piece of paper, allowing all of your negative *thoughts* and *feeling* to flow through your pen and out onto the page. Then, when you have finished writing your statement, see yourself reading it through before moving onto the next part of the exercise.

Then, in your mind's eye, visualize yourself either folding that piece of paper up as small as you can, or scrunching it up into a tiny ball. Then, as if you could, throw that piece of paper up into the air and over your head behind you. Throw it as hard as you can so that it will take off into space and create distance between you, and it.

As you imagine the paper with all of the negative thoughts and feeling attached to it taking off behind you, notice how it gets smaller and smaller until you can no longer see it. You can now take a deep sigh of relief knowing that it will never be seen again. As the distance gets greater between you and it, the negative thoughts and feelings associated with the goal will automatically become detached from yourself as well as your present positive move towards goals.

If you prefer you can actually physically write the statement down on a piece of paper, and then read it through before burning, shredding or disposing of it. Make sure that you only focus on the negative aspects, thoughts and feelings surrounding the goal and not the goal itself.

A Word About Positive Thinking And The Law Of Attraction

For many years we have been led to believe that as long as we think positively and we focus on our goals that we will be able to achieve anything. Sadly after much frustration and disappointment many of us came to the realization that this is not necessarily the case.

Later, we were delivered a very similar message which spoke of a gift from the universe that would allow us to *attract* or *manifest* anything we want into our lives. But still most of us failed to benefit from this concept too. So yet again many of us started to doubt the possibilities and some even gave up hope.

So why then, with all of these disappointments and unfulfilled promises are we still being told that we can attract anything into our lives just by thinking positively? And, if this is true, does this mean that we *are* truly attracting or manifesting everything into our lives just by thought?

In my opinion, I think not. Because if that was the case then I truly believe that there would be hundreds of millions of people living on this planet who would be living a very different life to what they are living today.

So then the questions that so many of us have, are, first is there really any truth behind the concept of positive thinking? And secondly, can the law of attraction actually assist *me* in achieving my goals? The answer is yes to both. But, they may not work in the way that we think they do, nor will they work in the way that we have been led to believe. However, if you chose to think about, and apply these concepts in the way that I am about to explain them to you, then not only might these concepts make more sense and seem more believable, but by applying them in this manner you may also start to experience a lot more success.

Let's start with the idea of positive thinking and how we can realistically apply it to our own lives in order to help us achieve our goals. First of all, we have to get it out of our heads that positive thinking alone will get us what we want. It is merely a way of thinking and not a whole process in which we can achieve success. In fact the idea of positive thinking alone can become a real trap and will probably set you up for failure.

In saying this, it is very useful to think positive, or at least some of the time, because we do need to be *realistic* too. If we look back to how we created our move towards, or positively stated goals we will realize that it is often by becoming aware of our negative thoughts and feelings that we are able to then figure out what we really want instead. However, upon realizing what it is that we do want, and stating it in the *positive*, it is then necessary to keep those *positive* thoughts in our awareness so that we can think about how we are going to achieve our goal.

Also, if we run into potential problems in life, or when we are trying to achieve our goals, we have to be realistic and objective in order to find the solutions we need to move forward. Thinking that we can simply wish everything well, or that if we think positively everything will work out just fine will probably cause us to become stuck. In fact this way of thinking is neither very realistic, nor is it a proactive approach to achieving any sort of success.

As for The Law of Attraction, the truth is that it actually does work, but again, it just might not work in the way that so many of us have often been led to believe that it does. It is not some new age gimmick nor is it a magic pill. It is though, based on the premise that whatever we put our attention on we will attract or manifest into our lives.

This might sound a bit misleading as it does make it sound a little bit like we can expect to get some sort of magical result just by thinking about whatever it is that we want. But if you believe that this is all that you have to do, which unfortunately so many people have been misled into believing, then you could be setting yourself up for failure yet again.

Anyone can utilize the law of attraction but you *must* understand that it is only *one* of the tools needed in order to achieve your goals. The key to having it assist you in becoming successful in any area of your life may actually have less to do with the concept of wishful thinking, and far more to do with creating awareness in your life, or around any part of it that you would like to experience change.

Having this awareness would mean that you would become clear about exactly what it is that you would like to achieve in your life, and then when you have done so, you will then also need to become aware of just how you are going to achieve it. The concept of attracting or manifesting something into your life works more like this.

So let's think about the Law Of Attraction for a moment. Statements which are often used with regards to this concept would be something like, whatever you put your attention on you will get more of, whatever you focus on you will attract into your life, or whatever you think about most will become your reality. Or, if you deliberately think about, and put your attention on whatever it is that you want in your life, you will then be able to manifest it.

Statements such as this sound so simplistic, but does this mean that this is all you have to do? Unfortunately there has been a lot of bad information out there that would lead you to believe this is so. But the law of attraction may actually work more like this.

Let's say that you love red roses. If you think about them and focus all of your attention on them does this mean that they will suddenly appear in your life? I don't think so. What it does mean is that because you really like them you will be far more likely to notice them whenever they are around. So, let's say that you are walking past a flower shop and there are hundreds of different types of flowers in the window including some red roses. Which flowers do you think are going to be the ones to catch your eye? Most likely the roses, right? And since you are so in tune with them because you love them so much, the smell of them may even stand out for you too. You may even decide to stop for a minute, to smell the roses.

This can happen with anything, such as when a guy loves a certain type of car. He will probably stop and take notice whenever one drives past him on the street. And if he is keen enough he may buy magazines to read up on them, or research them on the internet. But does this mean that if he puts enough attention on these cars that he will eventually manifest one into his life. Not in the way that it sounds, as in, I doubt that he will wake up one day to find one had magically appeared in his driveway.

What it does mean though is that if he loves the car enough, and he thinks that he would love to have one, he may decide to make this his goal. Then with the fact that he now knows what he wants, he will probably become inspired to find ways of how he could get one. And the more his desire grows will probably mean that he will also become more motivated and will take the action necessary to make sure he ends up with one of these cars.

So the question is then, is it the positive thinking and the fact that he is putting so much of his attention on what he wants that is going to manifest the car into his life? Or is it the fact that he is now fully aware of what he wants, and that he is so inspired that he has found creative ways of thinking and planning, and has become motivated enough to take the action necessary to achieve his goal?

The exact same thing can happen in any area of your life, including when you want to meet a partner or be with a certain person. If you think about this person all of the time and dream about him or her every night, it is not necessarily going to mean that you are going to attract this person into your life.

In order to do that you are going to have to take action, meaning that you will need to find out what it is going to take to get his or her attention, and for you to make an excellent impression. Then you will need to actually take action based on this information, and that will probably mean that you will also have to do some pursuing and ask that person out. And then you will need to keep working at wooing and pursuing. That is the way that you attract someone into your life.

The law of attraction can work in both positive and negative ways, and also carries with it the saying, whatever we resist persists. This means that even if we are thinking about or paying attention to something that we do not like, or do not want in our lives then the mere fact that we are putting our attention on that negative experience will keep attracting more of the same.

A good example of this would be when we want to lose that 20lbs. We may hate the way we look and feel about ourselves and we may desperately want to lose the weight. But if we keep focussing on the problem, being the 20lbs or the things we do not like about ourselves we will probably remain stuck. And thinking of the present state, which we are not happy with, will cause it to become a bit of a self fulfilling prophecy.

A lot of people in this situation will decide that they are going to lose the weight, (positive thought) and will think about taking action. Then they may go out and buy a gym pass (positive action) and put on their gym clothes before taking one look in the mirror and thinking, hang on a minute I'm not going to gym looking like this, I look way to fat in these clothes (whoa! very negative thought). Then perhaps feeling depressed about it, they decide to put off going for a few weeks which will give them chance to go on a diet and hopefully lose a few pounds in the meantime (very negative action). This is no joke! But people do this type of stuff all of the time. And in the meantime they put their life on hold, hence attracting more of the same, or *staying* the same as the case may be. They are essentially stuck at this point, mostly because they are not fully aware of, or fully in control of their thoughts.

The point I'm trying to make is that our thoughts have so much power over us even if we are not fully aware of what we are thinking half of the time. But as long as we are aware of what thoughts are going through our heads, we can change them. Remember, awareness is key!

Awareness is a very powerful tool. It gives us clarity, flexibility and choice. And it is perhaps this awareness and not the simple act of positive thinking or just putting our attention on whatever it is that we want, that will allow us to make the right decisions and take the right actions which are necessary in order for us to succeed.

There Is No Secret To It, You Have To Take Action If You Want To Succeed

There is only so much planning and positive thinking a person can do before there comes a point in time where we just *have* to take action. After all, no matter how committed we are to a goal, or how determined we are to achieve it, we still must take action in order to reap the rewards.

Some of us love to take action, and when we do we are usually driven to succeed. Then as long as we start to see some results it is very likely that we will remain motivated and continue on to achieve our goals. However, if on the other hand we do not see results fast enough or we are not getting the results that we wanted, we may lose our motivation and give up on the thing we were striving for.

Others may have more difficulty taking action and instead spend too much time in the planning stage. When this happens there is a very good chance that either they are not fully committed to doing the actual work involved in achieving their goal, they have some sort of fear present or there is some obstacle or objection looming in the background.

Perfectionists can remain stuck in this place for a very long time as they often feel that either they or their idea is not quite good enough. They may fear that they will meet disapproval from others, or they simply have to get all of their ducks in a row. In other words, perfectionists often make the mistake of waiting for the perfect time, which of course doesn't always come.

Then there are those people who simply never get their goals off the ground. And when this happens it can be an extremely frustrating way to live. The chances are someone who is stuck in this state probably lacks awareness of what is keeping them there.

If you are one of these people, then my advice would be to first read through the entire book to see if you recognize any habits, thoughts, feeling or behaviours which could be keeping you stuck. Then work through the entire program while focussing on some very simple goals. This will allow you to develop some healthy goal achievement skills, and you will get to experience some success with achieving your goals. This in turn will help you to build confidence in yourself, as well as around your abilities to achieve your goals. This is after all what this book is actually all about.

From here on I am going to try to keep the process clean, crisp and straight to the point, but I cannot reiterate this point enough, to achieve your goals you absolutely *have* to take action.

Pick A Goal And

Create Your Vision

Now, I know the last thing that I said was that you absolutely *have* to take action. BUT, and yes that is a very big BUT, before you go running off in all directions and taking all sorts of action, you need to know exactly what action you want or need to take. And the only way you will ever know this is by knowing exactly what you want to achieve.

You don't want to become one of those people who are so busy taking action that you don't have time to actually achieve your goals. Believe it or not millions of people make this mistake.

Knowing this, it is time to choose a goal and create your vision of exactly what you want to achieve. But this is where you also need to become aware of one of those hidden motivational strategies I was talking about. It is the Big Picture Versus The Little Picture Syndrome. Yes, I just made that name up. But this is one of those internal strategies that we are often unaware of, and yet it can have the power to either help or hinder our success.

As I keep saying awareness gives you power and choice. So I am going to explain how this works so that you will be able to use it to your benefit. If you chose to ignore these motivational strategies they will continue to run in your mind anyway and may cause you a lot of grief. However by becoming aware of them you will be able to harness their power and instead use them as incredible tools to help you succeed. Here's what this awareness strategy looks like.

When we think about a goal we will likely think about the big picture, or what we ultimately want to achieve, I'm going to call this our vision. Our vision is what we want to strive for. It will inspire us and give us the motivation to succeed. However, if we only focus on our big picture goal, or our vision, and we do not pay any attention to the details, we may have difficulty in figuring out how we are going to achieve our goal.

On the other hand, some of us are very detail oriented and good at breaking down and creating a lot of mini goals. However, if we become so focussed on achieving one of those mini goals, we could possible get side tracked and lose sight of our vision, which could actually cause us to forget what we are doing this all for. And, we could even end up losing our motivation or completely give up on our goal.

The difficulty of not being aware of our own visual patterns is that we could end up relying on only one of them, and this could ultimately prevent us from achieving our goal.

However, knowing this will allow us to see the benefit of being aware of both of our big picture goal which is our vision, and our little picture goals which are our mini goals or action step so that we can utilize them together and use them to our advantage.

We need to become aware of, and remain aware of our goals and our visions around the goals at all times. And that means we need this awareness during the planning stage of how we are going to achieve our goals, as well as throughout our entire goal achievement process. This way we can constantly check in with both our vision and our action steps to keep us on track and moving in the right direction.

Keep in mind that our Vision or Big Picture Goal and our Mini Goals work in harmony as a team. Our Big Picture Goal will provide our motivation, and our Mini Goals will keep us on track.

Create Your Vision And Design Your Big Picture Goal

It is now time to move forward by creating your big picture or vision around your goal. Remember this will become your motivation to succeed so you will want to make it as clear and as enticing as possible.

As you are creating your vision, if you find that you have feelings of self doubt about being able to achieve the goal, or if you have negative self talk in your mind, or even if you become aware of any obstacles or objections which you have around achieving the goal, just set them aside for the time being. We will be dealing with these issues as we work through the book.

For now your goal is to create your vision. Think of your vision as a reward or a prize that you will receive as a result of achieving your goal. Remember, this is your opportunity to create a picture in your mind of exactly what you want to achieve. It doesn't matter whether or not you believe you can do it at this point, just create your vision.

When doing so, be sure to use all of your senses and make this vision as real and as positive as possible. Be creative. You can make this picture in your mind as perfect as you like, so ask yourself these following questions. In a perfect world if I succeed at achieving my goal what will it look like? How will I feel? How will I experience this part of my life differently?

Here are some examples of question that you might use to create your vision of your ultimate goal:

Let's say that your goal is that you want to lose 20lbs. Visualize yourself as you will look when you have achieved your desired weight. Think about what you would love to look like. Notice the shape of your body. See how you might carry yourself differently and think about what clothes you will wear. Notice how people will respond to you, what will they say? How will they compliment you?

See how much more confidence you will have and how many ways your life might improve. What about your energy level, how will you feel? What new things might you want to try when you have more energy and confidence? Are there any new activities that you would like to do? If you are single will your new look inspire you to get out dating more often or perhaps commit to a relationship? How will you achieving your goal improve your health? Who else will benefit from your new level of confidence and energy? Notice all of the things that you will like better about yourself or your life after achieving your goal. Think about all of the ways your life might improve as a result of you losing these 20lbs.

Think about what you might do differently at your new weight, what new activities might you try, or how will it impact your health. How will you feel about yourself, how will you feel physically? What will you hear others say to you? What new foods might you discover and enjoy during and after the time that you lose weight.

Using these and any other questions or ideas you may already have, start to create your vision around your goal. Make it as clear and detailed and inspiring as possible. If you are a visual person it may help to create a collage. If you would rather journal then write about all of the positive ways your life will be different as a result of achieving your goal. Just start by brainstorming and then you can organize your thoughts later.

When you have finished this exercise, start to brainstorm about how you will go about achieving your goal, and what actions you will need to take in order to achieve it. Make a list of these actions as they will probably become mini goals or action steps for success.

Let's use another example about wanting to meet someone special to develop a relationship with. Again if you get any doubting thoughts, negative self talk in your mind or obstacles or objections just set them aside for now. The goal here is to create a fantastic vision, or big picture in your mind of you having achieved your goal.

Ask yourself the following question: If you were to meet the love of your life today, how would your life be different? How would you be spending your time? What are some of the things you would love to do with your new partner? Where would you go? What would it be like having someone in your life? What new things might you want to try together? List all of the things that would be more enjoyable with that one special person. What new emotions might you experience? What might that person be like? How will having a partner in your life positively affect your health? What about your emotional health? How might your living situation change for the better? How would having a partner change your future?

You could come up with endless questions, and may have already come up with endless ideas of how and why you would like to have that someone special in your life.

Gather all of this information and create a fantastic vision of your ultimate goal. Make it as positive and enticing as possible. Run through all of the positive scenarios in your mind and then fantasize about how life could be different in as many ways possible. Be sure to only focus on the positive.

Again, when you have finished this exercise, start to brainstorm about how you will go about meeting and attracting this person into your life. What actions will you need to take in order to achieve this goal? Make a list of these actions as they will probably become mini goals or action steps for success.

When you have completed your big picture goal, ask your subconscious mind to continue generating thoughts and feeling associated with achieving your goal. You can always go back and add to your vision at any time you want.

When you have finished gathering all of this information, write a statement about what you want to achieve and how you are going to achieve it.

Now that you have created your vision, going back to the S in SMART Goals, you have now turned your already Stated In The Positive Goal, into a very Specific Goal as well.

Connecting With And Attaching Yourself To Your Goal

Some people are experts at setting goals. They may know exactly what they want, and how they are going to get it. And they may be so determined to achieve their goal that they refuse to let anything get in their way.

These people are often willing to do whatever it takes to succeed and vow to do anything and everything in their power. And they may be so interested in achieving their goal that it may rank as a 10 on the scale of importance and priorities. They are driven to succeed, and are 100% committed to success, and are often so excited about achieving their goal that they can actually feel it throughout their bodies.

Some people may even have all of the skills, support and tools needed to bring their goal to life, and believe in themselves as well as their goals so much that they have no doubt in their minds about their ability to achieve what they want.

Many great goal setters can even have the most amazing vision for which they use to create their motivational big picture goal, and they methodically plan every step of the way. Then, for reasons which may seem beyond their control, or that they just can't seem to comprehend, they hit a wall causing them to suddenly stop still in their tracks as if they had became paralyzed by fear.

Then no matter how much they think about what they want to achieve or how badly they want to achieve it, they just can't seem to bring themselves to follow through. And that is it.... THE END. End of story. And all of their good intentions and brilliant goals, dreams, aspirations and often even their New Year Resolutions end up on the pile of unfulfilled goals.

Then defeated and doomed they try to rationalize why they just can't seem to bring these goals to life. This is one of the most disappointing places be. I have experienced this myself. And I know that no matter how frustrating it can become, or how badly we beat ourselves up, it is as if the whole process of goal setting falls flat on its face. And if we experience this often enough it can seem as if we really are doomed.

This is actually a very common scenario. It can affect anyone no matter how smart you are or motivated you appear to be. And unless you can figure out why you hit this wall that stopped you in your tracks, it can continue you sabotage you for years. This is also a classic cause for recurring goals. And the only thing that could be worse than getting caught in this rut is the fact that for the most part, most of us still desperately and genuinely still do want to achieve our goals.

So the question is this, why do we go so far and then all of a sudden quit? It doesn't make any sense especially when someone is so clear about what they want to achieve and so determined to get it.

There are probably several factors which cause this phenomenon. However, I believe that one of the main causes for so many people to not follow through with their goals is because they are simply not connected with, or attached to their goal.

By saying this, I mean that very often when it comes to taking action and turning our goal in to a reality, a person may suddenly realize that they are standing in this place and time with an image of this fantastic goal in their mind, but it actually *feels* as though it is nothing more than a dream. Or it may seem as though our vision is so far off in the distance that it is out of our reality. It may seem as though the goal is *out of our reach*.

When this happens it is often because we have no connection to the goal or no attachment to it. In other words we are disconnected from our goal. We are not associated with it. And for many of us, unless we have some sort of connection to our goal we may never actually be able to make it become a reality. This then means that we will need to find a way to connect with, attach ourselves to, or associate ourselves with our goal on a physical, mental and emotional level. And we can do this by using the following visual exercises.

At this point you should have created your vision or big picture of your goal. If you have not already done so, then you absolutely need to do this in order to complete this exercise.

When you have done so, you will then need to think of a way that you would like to become physically, mentally and emotionally connected to your vision. And, you may also want to see this connection as a way in which you can also bring your goal in closer to yourself, or move yourself closer towards your goal.

I have decided to use the image of a silver cord which has one end attached to myself and the other attached to the end of an arrow. If you do not want to do this exact visualization exercise, you can create one of your own which you can relate to. Just make sure that it will give you the same result, which is to make a connection between you and your goal.

The first time that you do this exercise, do it as if you are watching yourself doing the exercise in its entirety. You could even imagine that you are watching yourself doing this exercise on a big movie screen.

Now, see yourself standing in a very well lit aeroplane hangar which is lit with lighting for a film or photo shoot. Remember, you are the star of your own movie here. On the ground in front of you there is a golden bow and arrow and a long sliver cord with one end attached to the arrow and the other end tied around your waist.

Then as you watch yourself up on the screen you will see yourself picking up the bow and arrow and setting the arrow in the bow. Then, as if you could, continue to watch yourself on the screen as you look out into the distance where you will see your goal front and center in front of you.

Looking straight at your goal and seeing it in all of its might, draw back the arrow and fire it straight out in front of you and directly at the goal. Don't worry about your archer skills. This is a visualization exercise so you know that your arrow is going to hit your target straight on and plant itself firmly into your goal. You can now see that you are now physically attached to your goal.

As you see the silvery cord attached to both yourself and your goal you can be assured that you will remain attached physically, mentally and emotionally to your vision and your goal at all times. And as time passes you will become more mentally and emotionally connected with it.

Now repeat the exercise, only this time instead of seeing yourself in the picture you are going to experience the visualization as if you were actually there doing the exercise in real life and in present time.

This time it is as if you are actually right there in the aeroplane hangar and you are in your own body standing there looking directly out at your goal. You have a clear view and can see the goal right there in front of you. Now, look at the bow and arrow on the ground in front of you. When you are ready pick it up.

Notice how the bow and arrow feel in your hands, and feel the texture of the silver cord which is attached to the end of the arrow. Run the cord through your hands until you have reached the very end of it and tie the cord around your waist. Notice how it glistens. Feel the energy which is emanating from the cord.

With the cord now securely tied around your waist, set the arrow in the bow, draw back the arrow, aim and fire it directly at the goal in front of you.

Again, you have a perfect score with the arrow planting itself directly into your goal. You are now attached to your goal. And as you proceed to move forward you will remain attached physically, mentally and emotionally to your goal and you will become more associated with it.

The reason why we do this exercise twice and from different perspectives is because we need to be able to see the benefit of flipping back and forth between being associated and being dissociated. This skill will give us much more flexibility.

The first time we did the exercise we did it from the perspective of being dissociated, meaning that we watched ourselves going through the motions as if it was a mini movie of us firing the arrow at the goal. It is good to dissociate when we want to detach ourselves from the emotional aspects of a goal. This will allow us to step back so that we can see the whole picture without being emotionally involved. This position can allow us to think clearer.

When we did the exercise the second time we were associated, as if we were actually doing the exercise in real life, and in real time. The benefit of becoming associated with a goal is that it will seem more real, as if it is a part of us and that we are well and truly connected with the goal. This is a good place to be when we want to bring the goal to life and stay motivated by it.

Visual exercises such as this and others which you will find throughout the book can play a huge role in our lives, and they can really help us to succeed with anything.

You can do this exercise as many times as you want. And as you develop your mini goals or action goals, I would encourage you to do the same visual exercise with them too.

Motivational Strategies

If you are not convinced that you will do whatever is necessary to achieve your goals, then consider the following options.

Let's use the example of wanting to lose 20lbs. At this point you should have created a very enticing vision of what you want to look and feel like upon losing the weight. And you probably have some good ideas about how life could be more rewarding with having achieved your goal. This should be a very powerful move towards, motivational goal. Let's call this your Future Experience.

Now think about where you are today in your present state of mind, having your present experience, and thinking and feeling about wanting to lose the weight. Ask yourself the following questions:

What made you decide that you should, or want to lose the weight? How do you feel? What do think about yourself and the way that you look? What is it about your current weight that you do not like? Who or what do you avoid because of your present weight? How does this excess weight affect your life? Do you like the way you look or feel? Do you have the energy, flexibility and stamina that you would like? Do you like the way your clothes fit or the style of the clothes you wear? Do you feel as vibrant and outgoing as you could be? Are you the best possible version of yourself right now? How else does your excess weight affect your physical, mental or emotional health or lifestyle? Let's call this your Present Experience.

Now as you think about your Present Experience, notice how it makes you feel. Then move your attention back to your Future Experience, how does that make you feel? Ask yourself the following question: In a perfect world which experience would you rather have?

If when thinking about your future experience you have any thoughts of self doubt or you experience negative chatter in your mind, or if any obstacles or objections come up for you, just set them aside for now as we will be doing some exercises to help deal with them a little later in the book. And, again think about which experience you would rather have on a daily basis.

Now consider this. If one year from now you have not taken the action necessary to achieve your goal, do you think that your life will be better, worse or the same?

The chances are it could be the same. However if you look back one year from today and realize that you have let yourself down and that you have had the time to make your goal a reality but you didn't follow through, you could very well be feeling a whole lot worse. Because if you don't follow through there will be a very good chance that you will feel even more disappointed and frustrated with yourself than you do today. And, you will probably also be kicking yourself for not succeeding at your goal.

On the other hand, if one year from now you have achieved your goal and you are experiencing all of the amazing rewards which come along as a result of achieving it, there is a very good chance that you will be feeling pretty amazing about yourself. And you will have the added bonus of feeling very proud of your accomplishments. Give power to your Future Experience. Spend time every day thinking about all of the positive ways your life will change by having this Future Experience.

Your destiny is in *your* own hands. You get to chose whether or not *you* will achieve this goal. So my question is, are *you* willing to, and will *you*, take the action necessary to achieve this goal? Remember, you absolutely have to take the necessary action if you want to succeed.

Creating The Identity Of A More Empowered You

When we want to experience change in our life, which will likely mean achieving some goals, it is important that we believe on both a conscious and unconscious level that we can, and will do whatever it is going to take. This may mean that even though we may *think* that nothing will get in our way, deep down inside we may not actually *believe* that we can or will achieve our goal. And this may be especially true if the belief does not fit in with our subconscious mind, or if it does not fit in with our identity.

Whether we realize it or not our identity can keep us stuck. And even though our identity is who we believe we are, because it is so hardwired into our own personal programming, we are usually not even consciously aware of how it can affect us. Neither do we typically give it much thought.

However, because our identity is such an integral part of our programming we will usually do whatever it takes to live up to it. Meaning that, no matter how much we might want to change, or how different we want to be, we will typically default to going back to, and *doing* whatever it takes to maintain our present identity.

So, with this said, the problem which often arises whenever we want to experience some sort of change in our life is when that change, will require a shift in our personal identity. Such as needing to see ourselves in a different way, or behaving in a different way to what we have always done in the past. However, because our old beliefs and behaviours are often so well ingrained, they may be difficult, *but not impossible,* to change.

Knowing this then it is important that whenever we want to achieve such a goal that we become aware of, and tweak our identity so that it includes any positive new changes we want to make in our life.

It is not only important to achieve the goal but it is also important that we can identify with having achieved it. So often when we create a goal it can be difficult to believe that we can achieve it if it means that our identity of ourselves does not fit with the identity of having achieved the goal. And this conflict often happens on an unconscious level, meaning that it is not fully in our awareness, so on a conscious level we may think that we can achieve a particular goal, but our subconscious mind does not believe it.

For example let's say that you want to be financially successful but you have always had struggles with money. Your current identity *may* be that you have been, or that you are poor, or broke.

Now let's say that you set your goal to earn a ton of money. And you know that you want to succeed more than anything else in the world. If your internal subconscious identity tells you that you are a poor person, then you may very well have a more difficult time believing deep down inside, or seeing yourself in any other way. This may mean that it will be more of a challenge to succeed. However, if you had the ability to install a new belief into your identity which would help your subconscious mind align itself with your conscious awareness, then it could very well make your achievements easier.

Here is a great visualization exercise to help you create a more powerful identity associated with achieving your goal.

Creating A New Identity

Wouldn't it be nice if we could create a program which would allow us to become anything that we wanted to be, or to achieve anything that we wanted in life, and then we could install it into our subconscious mind, just like you would with a computer program? Hmmm!!!

The next step to creating the new more powerful and resourceful you, is to integrate your new image into your subconscious mind so that this change becomes believable on a mind/body level. We are going to do this with a visualization exercise.

The reason I think it is so important to do this part of the process is that if we have developed a lot of negative behaviours and patterns in our life we will eventually believe that is who we are. I experienced this after suffering with anxiety and debilitating panic attacks.

At the time my anxiety and panic attacks were so bad that my life had all but shrivelled up to a mere existence, and I was no longer able to do so many of the things I had previously done. I was so desperate to get my life back that I researched and experimented with all sorts of alternative therapies which eventually helped me to overcome the symptoms. However, because I had avoided doing so many things for so long, I developed the belief that I could no longer do them. And even though in my mind I desperately wanted to live my life to the fullest, I just couldn't follow through.

After a great deal of contemplation I realized that the very thing which was now holding me back was the identity that I had now developed of having the anxiety and panic attacks and the belief that I could no longer do certain things. And even though I had all but overcome the anxiety and panic attacks I still could not do them. With this is mind I decided to create a new identity of myself becoming the person I wanted to be. And this meant that I also decided that I wanted to become unstoppable, as in having the courage to do anything I wanted. Then, after I had created my new identity, I also created a visualization exercise similar to this one to help me install it.

I have created the following exercise especially for the purpose of building confidence.

Creating A Powerful Version Of Yourself - Visualization Exercise

Think for a moment about the person, or version of yourself that you want to become after having achieved your goal. Get into that state, or frame of mind and imagine exactly what it will be like.

Next, imagine that you are standing under a street lamp when you notice someone walking towards you. This person is confident, reassured, and looks as though they really "have it together." It is someone who you admire and *who* you aspire to be just like. Looking hard you can tell that this person has all of the qualities and characteristics that are on your wish list, and that are needed to achieve your goals.

In the darkness, you cannot see precisely who this person is but you sense a certain familiarity. Struggling to see who it is walking towards you, you sense a certain excitement, and feel at ease with their presence. That perfect stranger walking towards you is somehow giving you strength, hope and a sense of power. As they approach you feel confident and empowered, and you can feel the positive feelings that you know you will experience when you have achieved your goal.

Now as this person approaches the light, you notice that he or she is really happy, content and confident, and has become the person *you*, now aspire to be. You feel that happiness and contentment too. In fact you can feel the confidence and all of the feelings you hope to experience.

Now, as you take a step towards this empowered and confident stranger you can feel the energy, strength and confidence they exude. Then, as this person reaches the street light which is now shining down onto both of you, you recognize who it is. With a feeling of happiness, joy and pride, you take a deep breath as you realize that the perfect stranger is in fact…. YOU!

Take a moment to connect with this vision and savour these feelings of your success.

As you are doing this exercise, use your own list of powerful and positive emotional resources that you would like to integrate into your mind/body system, and attach them to the person in your visualization. Repeat the exercise frequently; adding more powerful emotional resources each time you do it. Also see yourself getting closer and closer to the vision until you eventually become at one with it.

Take pride in knowing that you are now taking the steps to achieve your goals and make your dreams come true. Just by recognizing and admitting what you want to achieve in life you have started the process of becoming that person which you desire to be.

You can gain confidence, you can gain strength, you can change the way you look, the way you feel, the way you dress and the way you respond to others; you can live any life you want to live. You can continue to reinvent yourself by adding any new and powerful resources that you would like to add to your life. You can constantly be reinventing yourself until you become the person you really want to be. Why not become the best version of yourself possible?

Powering Up Your Goals

If you are experiencing any sort of hesitation with one of your goals, ask yourself the following question. Be completely honest with yourself here. Are you willing to, and will you commit to taking the action necessary in order to achieve your goal? Will you commit to doing the work required to succeed?

If the answer is yes, then go for it. If your answer is no, then first ask yourself if you really do want to achieve this goal, is it really important enough to you. Then either spend some time trying to figure out what is preventing you from achieving it, or do the following exercise to power up your goal.

Then while thinking back to your vision or your big picture goal, and reviewing all of the positive things that you will experience by having achieved it, do the exercise in chapter 4, to rank the goal for importance and priority.

Ask yourself, what number would a goal need to rank at, in order for you to know for sure, with 100% certainty, that you will follow through and do whatever it takes to achieve this goal. Then upon doing the exercise if your goal ranks at a number which falls below the number which you just stated, ask yourself what is it going to take in order to bring that goal up to meet your required number. This should bring up some very important information for you although it might not come to you right away. Then when you have figured this out, ask yourself, what would it take, for that goal to rank as a 10 on the scale of importance and priorities.

Reconnect With Your Vision And Draw It In Closer To You

Now looking into the distance and towards your vision, see your goal out there in front of you. Imagine the goal as if it were like a big fluffy cloud which is suspended in the air, with the ability to float quite freely. Thinking back to the exercise where you attached yourself to your goal, once again imagine picking up the silver cord which is attached to both yourself and the goal in front of you, and give the cord a gentle tug. This will help to bring the goal in closer to you, and perhaps even a little more within your reach. Let this process absorb into your subconscious mind

Recognizing And Dealing With Obstacles, Objections and Conflicting Beliefs

Everyone, at some point in our lives will come to a time or place where we just feel stuck. We may feel stuck around a particular issue or around life in general. And when this happens, perhaps because we can become overwhelmed by our situation, and the negative emotions such as frustration which will probably surround it, we may have difficulty recognizing what is actually causing us to feel this way. However until we figure this out, it will probably be very difficult for us to see just what we need to do to get back out of this rut.

It doesn't matter who you are or what you do, we all have internal programs which run in the back of our minds so subtly that we might not even be aware that they are there. However no matter how deep they may be buried, or silent they may seem, these programs often have the power to control our lives. But until we bring them into our awareness and acknowledge them and give them the attention that they need, these programs will probably continue to attack, and attempt to sabotage us in whatever part of our life they hold power over us. These internal programs could even prevent us from achieving anything that we truly desire.

The programs I am referring to present themselves in the form of obstacles, objections and conflicting beliefs, and usually appear in the form of negative self talk, or even uneasy feelings and emotions. They can be so intrusive that we will want to ignore them altogether, but that would be the worst thing to do. In fact the best way to quell these internal saboteurs is by giving them some attention, as this will allow us to become aware of what we need to do in order to put them to rest.

These obstacles, objections or conflicting beliefs would likely have made themselves known to you in the form of those negative little voices in your head that say, yes but, or what if, or if only, or the problem is, or, *you* can't do that!. Or that those little voices that say things like, on one hand I want *this*, but on the other hand I want *that*. And they may even remind you of all of the reasons why you cannot or will not achieve your goals. And if you let them, they will push you right back into that negative territory where you could easily become bogged down, overwhelmed or even paralyzed by fear.

The best way to deal with these obstacles and objections is to give them some attention and find out what the underlying message is. We need to find out what is the positive intention behind the objection or conflicting belief

How To Recognize Your Self Sabotaging Internal Programs So That You Can Turn Them Into Allies

Internal Conflicts or Conflicting Beliefs

An internal conflict or a conflicting belief can cause chaos in our lives because having them usually means that we have two or more conflicting beliefs, needs or wants that clash with or oppose each other.

A good example of an internal conflict would be when someone says that they want to settle down and get married, but then again, they don't want to give up their single life. Or when someone claims that they desperately want to lose weight, but they are not willing to take the actions necessary in order to make it happen.

These internal conflicts can crop up in almost any area of our lives and often sabotage our best intentions. And this may mean that even though we have these conflicting thoughts, in reality, the thing that we truly do want to experience is some sort of positive change.

Using the examples above, that would mean the person really does want to get married, or to lose weight. However since making this change will likely require more awareness and effort on our part, and since as humans we often take the path of least resistance, we may unconsciously chose to, or simply continue to, live our life using the same habits that we have already created and that we have become comfortable with in our lives.

These habits can cause us to become complacent or can even keep us stuck. And this is where we will probably remain until we once again become aware of our present experience, being that we feel lonely so we start thinking about marriage again, or that we feel uncomfortable with how we look and feel, so we start to think about losing weight again. It will be the pain, or discomfort which is associated with our thoughts and feelings which surround that area of our life that we would like to experience change which will probably inspire us to once again start thinking about what we want to experience instead. And the cycle of wanting to experience change starts all over again. This is how we end up with recurring goals.

Dealing with these internal conflicts or conflicting beliefs is an extremely important piece of the puzzle, because unless we do so, we may never take the action necessary to experience positive change. This would mean that it wouldn't matter if we had crystal clear, positive, move towards goals, a fantastic plan of action or tons of motivation. Unless we acknowledge and make amends with these internal conflicts we *may* never achieve or maintain our success.

Here is an excellent exercise to help you quell you internal conflicts and conflicting beliefs.

You will recognize an internal conflict when you find yourself saying, a part of me wants this, but another part of me wants that. In our example we might be saying a part of me wants to get married but another part of me enjoys being single, or is afraid of the commitment, or really doesn't want to have to make too much effort, whatever the case may be. So what we need to do is to unite these parts of us so that they support each other, and work in unison instead of against each other.

We have already established that these internal conflicts are like parts of ourselves. Now, as if you could, imagine yourself holding your hands out in front of you with your palms up. Then imagine holding these two individual parts or conflicts in the palms of your hands, one in each hand.

For example, in one hand you have that part of you which represents the idea, thought or feelings that you want to get married, and in the other you have the part which represents the idea, thoughts, feelings, or objection to getting married.

Looking at the hand with the idea of wanting to get married, ask what it wants with regards to wanting to get married? Wait for the response. Listen to the reasons, what thoughts and feelings are being generated, and come to mind.

Then, when you have an answer, thank that part of you for sharing. Then look to the hand with the conflicting belief and ask, what is the reason behind the conflict or objection, what has been or is preventing you from taking action? Listen for the answer. Be patient and just listen and observe patiently.

When you have the answer, thank that part of you for sharing. Looking back at the first hand, ask that part to acknowledge what has just been brought to your attention, and then to once again respond. Keep this communication open and respectful while keeping the dialogue between the two parts of yourself going back and forth until you have reached a good understanding and awareness of what is going on between these parts of you.

At the end of the exercise ask each of the parts if they would agree to work together to find a middle ground and positive solution. When you have gotten an agreement between the parts, bring your hands together, and draw them in towards your heart. Take a moment to allow the parts to come together.

The whole point of this exercise is to gain an understanding of where these thoughts and feelings are coming from, and what their purpose or positive intention is. You need to find this out, as this will probably reveal what has been preventing you from moving forward.

The reason why you bring these parts out in the open and hold them in the palms of your hands is so that you can detach the feelings from yourself, allowing free and non judged internal communication. This will allow the parts to work towards a peaceful resolution.

This is an amazing exercise, my clients love it. You just have to be very careful not to analyze the process. Just let it happen and let your subconscious do the work here.

Obstacles

Obstacles are part of everyday life. A typical obstacle that someone could run into when they want to achieve a goal would be lack of money, resources, or time. All that this means is that the obstacle needs to be taken into consideration, and probably looked at as a challenge which needs to be overcome. Simply put, you probably need to turn this obstacle into a goal, which we will call a secondary goal. Then you will need to put this secondary goal through the whole goal achievement process to see what you need to do in order to overcome the obstacle and move on.

In other words an obstacle is probably just another goal which you had not yet identified, or considered until this point. Take this new goal back to the beginning of the process, turn the obstacle into a move towards goal, and then use all of your goal achievement skills to overcome it. This is a great way to build strength, determination and power.

Weeding Out Objections And Obstacles

If you are not sure if you have any obstacles, objections or conflicting beliefs or if you don't know where they are coming from, ask yourself the following questions. These questions may or may not reveal such things, they may instead only help you to realize that you actually have more power and control over your success than you might have thought possible.

Ecology Check

This is a good exercise to see if there are any objections or obstacles preventing you from achieving your goal.

If you achieve this goal, who will it affect in either a positive or negative manner?

Who else besides yourself will be impacted or affected by you achieving this goal?

Who might possibly be able to help you achieve this goal?

Who might not be supportive or might not agree with you achieving this goal?

When do you think you will be able to achieve this goal?

What do you need in order to achieve this goal?

What might you have to give up in order to achieve this goal?

What might prevent you from achieving this goal?

What has stopped you from achieving this goal in the past?

What could stop you from achieving this goal now?

Where will you be able to achieve this goal?

How will you achieve this goal?

Maintaining Balance In Your Life While Achieving Your Goals, Dreams, Aspirations and New Year's Resolutions.

Very often when we set out to achieve a goal we can become so focussed, determined and motivated to achieve it that it can seem as though we lose our peripheral vision, and many of us even lose sight of what is most important to us. We may even disconnect from other parts of our life and the results can be devastating.

A good example of this would be when a very career oriented person puts so much time into their education or work that they lose track of time and people. Many men and women have experienced this after spending years of their life, chasing after their goals and material wealth only to find themselves waking up one day, and wondering what they have missed out on. And often questioning what they are doing it all for.

This happens because they often make the mistake of becoming so focused on their goal that they fall into the trap of ignoring or eliminating certain aspects of their life. And consequently end up compartmentalizing their lives so much that they lose sight of whom, or what they value most. Many of us will do this to the point that we put our lives on hold, but if we lose track of time we could end up doing this indefinitely. And this could be a very high price to pay for success.

If we ignore our health and wellness, put our love lives on hold, kid ourselves that we do not need a social life, or detach ourselves from community or our spiritual awareness, we run the risk of ending up lonely and alone. And by the time we become aware of our situation, and realize that the life we have created is simply not fulfilling enough, it can often be difficult to get back on track. And this is why we need to create and maintain balance in our life.

The whole point of having balance is to be aware of, and nurture and maintain all of the parts of our lives that are important to us and that make us who we are, or even more importantly who we want to become. This may mean that we need to pay attention to, and give time to nurturing and developing important relationships, spending time with family and friends, taking care of our health and fitness, being involved in our community or perhaps volunteering for a special cause. We may also want to practice some sort of spiritual awareness and personal growth, whatever that may mean to you. And, of course you can keep adding to the list.

Although it may seem difficult to achieve balance it will allow us to have it all, because without it, something is going to give. I do not know anyone who set out to be successful, alone, lonely, disconnected, unhealthy, bored and unfulfilled. However, I have met many who have unintentionally achieved this.

Balance is about being aware. Aware of who you are, what you want, what is important to you, and how you fit into the world around you. Or, what type of world you want to create and develop around you. It may seem that by having balance in our life it will take longer to achieve our goals, but without balance we may actually end up resenting our goals and even give up on them altogether. With this in mind then it would make sense to strive for a full and balanced life, at all times.

If you are not sure what it means to have, or how to have balance, start by writing a list of all of the areas of your life which are important to you. They may include such things as family, friends, relationships, community, spirituality, personal growth, hobbies, interests, work, play, career, travel. You can develop your own list.

Then after completing your list think about how much time you would like to devote to each area of your life and when you would like to do this. Also, consider how you will go about making sure that you will fulfill these commitments to yourself, the people in your life, and to the various areas of your life.

If you like you can start with a worksheet where you have nine boxes on it, and you will need to fill each box with an area of your life that you would like to devote some time too. Just remember to keep these priorities in your awareness, and practice devoting time to maintaining balance in your life on a daily, weekly and monthly basis.

Why Work With A Coach?

Very often when we have made the decision that we want to achieve a goal we feel so excited that we just can't wait to share our ideas with our family and friends. Our hopes are probably that we will gain both their approval as well as their support. However, if we are met with a lack of enthusiasm or worse yet some resistance, we may easily become discouraged and back down or even bail on our goals.

Most people find it very beneficial to have someone to talk to about their goals. Sometimes all we want to do is to think out loud knowing that there is someone there to hear us. Other times we may want or need someone else's input or perhaps some validation. But before we talk to anyone about our goals we should take a moment to consider whether we are an internally, or an externally motivated person. This is one of those hidden little factors that we need to be aware of.

What this means is that if we are internally motivated, we trust ourselves and are comfortable with making our own decisions, and we will stick with them no matter what others might say or think. And we will likely not be swayed by someone else's feedback or opinions. On the other hand, if we are externally motivated we may instead want or need the help and approval from someone else in order to make a decision. And we may even change our minds or perhaps give up on our goals in an effort to please someone else. It is important to know this about yourself.

If you are not sure which category you fall into, or how you react to other people's responses or opinions of you or your goals, consider how you would normally make a decision around an everyday occurrence. Let's just say when you want to buy a new article of clothing.

When you walk into the clothing store do you know what you like, or what looks good on you? And if so would you stick with your decision no matter what others may say? Or, do you wait for someone else to give you feedback, or make a suggestion then allow yourself to be talked out of something that you like. Or, only buy whatever that other person says suits you even though you might not necessarily think so yourself.

I use this analogy because I have worked as a fashion and image consultant and I have always been amazed at how so many people either do not know what looks good on them, or they are too afraid to express what they really like for fear of being judged. So they allow other people to make their decisions for them.

A good example of this is when someone tries on an outfit. You can tell how much they love it by the look on their face and how they hold themselves. However he or she will refrain from making a decision until they get approval from a friend. And will allow him or herself to be talked out of buying something without any sort of resistance at all. Sales people love these types of customers as they can also be easily influenced into buying anything that the salesperson tells them they look good in.

The bottom line is that if you like to make your own decisions then you are internally motivated. If you let someone else influence your decisions for you, then you are probably externally motivated. This is a very important fact to know about yourself before talking to anyone about achieving your goals because if you are externally motivated you will need to be extremely careful about who you share your goals and dreams with. Someone may unwittingly make a comment that could cause you to change your mind and this could mean that you could ultimately change you path in life.

It is likely that we all use both of these strategies from time to time. However, one of the dangers of being externally motivated is that we could end up giving up on, or changing our goals to please someone else. And that could mean that we would be allowing that other person to carve out our life, and consequently even our future.

I remember a time that I was obviously externally motivated even though I was not aware that there was such a thing. When I was about nineteen years old and working as a hairstylist, I was approached by someone who wanted to put together an artistic team to travel to Honk Kong and Japan to teach. They asked me if I would be interested in leading the team, and of course I was quite interested in the opportunity. I was so excited that I went home that night and called my uncle who travelled internationally with his work, as I was interested to know what he thought.

However, my excitement was immediately deflated when he responded by questioning why anyone would possibly want to come and see me teach hair, after all nobody even knew who I was. That was the end of my excitement. It ended with a phone call which stopped me in my tracks and put an end to my vision of becoming an international trainer. And I never even stopped to question why.

Obviously I was externally motivated at the time, but looking back I must have been looking for his approval and not just his opinion. This has always stuck with me and I have often questioned why I gave up so easily. But that would never happen now.

In saying this many people find that they want and need someone to support them with their goals and dreams. And they may need someone to help them to figure out a plan and to check in with them along the way, or even to help motivate them. But it is often better to share your goals and dreams with someone who has no personal agenda for you, and that may mean that you will need to hire a coach.

One of the problems so many of us encounter when we share our ideas with family and friends is that although deep down inside these people probably have our very best interests at heart, some may also unwittingly have their own agenda for us too.

Another thing to consider is that the people who we are closest to are usually comfortable with who we already are, and the thought of us making major changes in our life can cause them to feel threatened by the possibility that we could leave them behind.

Also, when the time comes that you need someone to challenge and motivate you to stay on track, a family member or a friend may not be completely comfortable to challenge you for fear of causing conflict or hurting your feelings. A friend will not likely want to cross any boundaries in order to challenge you for fear of it affecting your friendship. Besides, you are far more likely to slack off with a friend than you will with a coach who will keep you accountable. And since your goal is probably to achieve success while keeping your personal relationship intact, then you might want to consider bringing in an outsider in the form of a coach to help you succeed.

This is often a time when you need someone to confide in. Someone who will listen and not judge you, who has your best interest at heart, who has no agenda for you and who can inspire, empower and motive you. Someone you can collaborate with, who will encourage you and help you to clarify your goals and dreams so that you can bring them to life. This is when you need a coach.

Share your goals with your coach and your successes with your family and friends. Team up with a coach so that you can become the best version of yourself possible.

New Year Resolution Planner

Wouldn't it be fantastic if at the end of the year you looked back at your list of New Year Resolutions and realized that you had followed through and achieved each one? It is possible to do, especially if you create and follow a plan.

The following pages will help you to do just that, and they have been organized in a way to keep you on track with your New Year Resolutions, as well as to plan for, and break down each individual goal.

You will find copies of all of these worksheets on my websites www.suzanneprice.com or www.newyearresolutions.info

New Year Resolution Goals

The first thing that you will need to do is to make a list of your New Year Resolution Goals.

Personally, I like to work on my list during the week between Christmas and New Year's Eve as I like to go into the New Year with my list already intact. That way I feel as though I am ahead of the game and I am setting myself up for success.

This is one of the habits I have created for myself over the years as it was one of my New Year Resolutions. I wanted to become more organized with my time so I started to plan my day, week, month or year, or any goal ahead of the start date.

By planning ahead of time I actually get to start my projects on time instead of scrambling to plan during the time I feel I should be actually working on them, and then feeling as though I have fallen behind. I now feel so much more organized and there are also huge psychological rewards as I now know what I have to look forward too, and this relieves a lot of stress.

Start by brainstorming and creating a list of all of the goals, dreams, aspirations and New Year Resolutions that you want to achieve, or at least want to start working on this year.

You can always go back and add to your list later

New Year Resolution Goals   Completion Date

Monthly Goals

Now that you have your list of New Year Resolution Goals that you would like to work on during the upcoming year and you have specified your completion date, you can decide which goal or goals you want to start with first.

Some people like to spend time to plan out the entire year and decide which goals they want to work on each month. I personally like to plan each month as I go through the year. I simply keep my New Year Resolutions list at hand and then plan for each month as it approaches. Even though I do not like to set out my monthly goals for the whole year ahead of time, I still do like to plan each month during the last week of the month, prior to the one I will be working on. That way I can start the month with a clear vision.

Goals For The Month Of   Completion Date

Weekly Goals

Now that you know what you want to achieve for the upcoming month, you can either break down your list of goals for that month and create a week by week plan, which will allow you to see exactly what you need to accomplish by a particular date, or you can take the approach of planning each week as it approaches.

I usually like to plan each week as it approaches. However, if I have a specific goal or task which absolutely has to meet a very specific deadline, I am more likely to plan out what needs to be done for the entire month. That way I can make sure that the goal in question gets priority, and this will allow me to see if I need to bump things up a bit or reorganize my time.

Goals For The Week Of   Completed

Daily Goals

With your list of goals for the week ahead you can now write down the goals which you want to achieve on a daily basis. Again I usually do this each day, writing my list in the evening prior to when I am going to work on these goals.

I also make it a habit to read my list of goals first thing in the morning and spend a few minutes thinking them through. This way I know what my priorities will be for the day and I will be able to think about how or when particular things need to be done by.

The main purpose of planning in this way is to keep our goals in our awareness so that we don't find ourselves constantly missing out on things that we wanted to do or achieve.

I used to be extremely resistant to goal setting and planning and always lived very spontaneously. However, I would often find myself kicking myself or regretting the fact that I had missed out on something either because I had completely missed the event, or missed the deadline for signing up. This lack of awareness is a typical cause for recurring goals and it can create an awful lot of disappointment and stress.

Daily Goals & Actions   Completed

Acknowledging Your Successes And Bringing Any Obstacles Into Your Awareness

As you work through your goals and take steps towards achieving your New Year Resolutions there will probably be times when you feel as though you are either not making enough progress or that you have hit a wall.

The best thing to do at this point is to take a break for a couple of days if you can afford the time. And then take a good look at what is going on. A good way to do this is to dissociate yourself from the goal, just like you did in the exercise where you saw yourself up on a big screen with the bow and arrow. The reason why I suggest that you do this from a dissociated state is so that you detach yourself from any negative emotions surrounding the goal. This will allow you to step back and see the whole picture without being emotionally charged. However when you are ready to get back on track make sure that you reconnect with the goal and give power to your vision by paying attention to it.

You may also want to discuss where you are at with someone who you can trust such as a friend who is completely honest with you, and supportive of your goal. Or if you are working with a coach talk with him or her. Or if you prefer, write down some questions that you need answered and then think them through and answer them for yourself.

Start by first looking at the goal or area of your life which you feel is causing you some frustration. Then think about and write down what you have achieved, what *is* working, where you have made progress, and how far you have come.

I like to write my answers down because I can always go back and read them later and this will often help me realize that things are not as bad as they may seem when we are feeling stuck. I can also then see where I have actually made some progress.

And remember, even if you are not seeing a lot of progress, as long as you are taking action and taking steps towards achieving your goal you are still succeeding at strengthening your goal achievement habits.

When you have finished acknowledging your successes you then need to think about what questions you need answered; remember you are looking for solutions. Your questions should be something like: What is holding me back? What do I need to do in order to achieve this goal? What is it that I am really frustrated about?

The whole point of asking these questions is to bring into your awareness the reasons why you are having problems achieving your goals, as having this awareness you will help you to find a solution.

Be very careful here. One of the biggest mistakes that people run into in life and in relationships is when they ask questions about the problem, such as what went wrong? Then instead of finding a solution and focussing on resolving the problem and moving forward, they make the mistake of putting their attention on and focusing on what actually caused the problem. This will often keep a person stuck, sometimes even for years. Remember the saying, whatever you put your attention on you will get more of?

However if you ask a question which will bring the problem into your awareness, you will then be able to find and focus on the solutions. This is a good practice for self coaching.

S.M.A.R.T Goal Planner

This final exercise will allow you to complete the process of turning an individual goal into a S.M.A.R.T goal. You have already created a very specific goal which is stated in the positive. So you have your S covered.

Write your goal down on this page so that you can keep it present. Using the vision which you created, which is your big picture goal, describe it in as much detail as possible. Include all of the positive aspects of the goal and remember to use all of your senses. Visual – your vision, Kinaesthetic – how you feel about your goal, Auditory – what you might hear, Olfactory & Gustatory if they apply. And of course your sixth sense which is your gut feeling.

Create A Timeline

Now you need to create a timeline. First decide how much time you need, and can allow yourself to achieve your goal. Be realistic as you want to make sure that you will be able to achieve it. This will be the first step of making your goal, timely or tangible.

Then break the timeline down into weeks, months or days, and create a worksheet for each one of the time frames required to achieve your goal i.e. month, week or day Now you will have covered the T in your smart goal making it Timely.

On this page write down the date which you will start working on your goal, the date which you plan to have completed it, and how many weeks, months or days it is going to take you.

Create Mini Goals

Now that you have completed that step, you will need to break your goal down into smaller pieces, mini goals, or stepping stones. These smaller goals will help the goal become more manageable, realistic and achievable. This step will cover the A and the R in your smart goals, meaning that your goal will become more Realistic as well as Actionable.

On this page start making a list of all of the action steps you need to take in order to achieve your goal.

List Your Mini Goals

List Your Mini Goals

Allocate Your Mini Goals

Finally, you will need to allocate your mini goals, spreading them out over the duration of the timeline. Really think about what needs to be achieved as well as what aspects of the goal may require very specific deadlines in order to make the whole goal fall into place.

You may find that you will want to start off at the end of the timeline, at your deadline, and write down what the final steps for completing your goal will be. Then if there are any aspects of the goal which need to be done by a specific date, place them on the timeline in the appropriate place. Then fill in the space around these milestones with any other action steps of the goal.

This will help you to create a solid timeline which will allow the mini goals or stepping stones to also become Actionable, Realistic and Measureable. This will cover the M, A. and R of your S.M.A.R.T. goal as your goal is now also Measurable, Actionable and Realistic.

You will find individual goal planning sheets on my website www.suzanneprice.com or www.newyearresolutions.info

A Final Word

At this point you should have set some very clear, specific and realistic goals. You now need to achieve them, so it is time to move into action stage so that you can bring your goals to life. Start by connecting with your goal and then take action immediately.

Your success is in your own hands, if you run into an obstacle simply turn it into a mini goal and work through it with the same process. Be creative, come up with a solution, and keep moving forward.

If you ever find yourself feeling stuck and wanting to give up, or you are feeling a bit overwhelmed or even defeated, just take a deep breath and brainstorm. Constantly challenge yourself and give power to your vision of whatever it is that you want to achieve.

Pay attention to what you are saying to yourself, deal with that negative chatter by asking what it wants from you, then listen to what the messages are as this can often help you find the solution. And if you ever hear yourself saying something like, *something has got to change*, (I hear people saying this *all* of the time) remember that there is only one thing that has to change, and that thing, is *you*.

You need to change your mind and you need to focus on what you want, and then you also need to get into creative problem solving mode so that you can come up with some solutions to keep moving forward. Every little step will help you move towards what you want as long as you remain aware of what you are thinking and feeling, and you keep refocusing to get in tune with what you truly want, and YOU TAKE ACTION.

Good luck with achieving your goals, dreams, aspirations and New Year Resolutions.

You will find a step by step Goal Planner which will guide you through every step of this program, as well as downloadable copies of all of the worksheets on my websites www.suzanneprice.com or www.newyearresolutions.info

A Note From Suzanne on Passion, Purpose &

The Importance Of Goals.

After working extremely hard for many years and realizing that life was not going the way I had envisioned, I often wondered if this was as good as it was going to get. I had been self employed, held down second jobs, and yet I still was not reaping the rewards.

So I completely put my personal life on hold, worked even harder and seemed to be constantly taking courses to better myself. Now even more focused on my career, and feeling completely unfulfilled, I finally realized that I had become one of those people who had compartmentalized my life so much, that all I seemed to be doing with my life was going to work.

I felt extremely stuck, and I lacked passion and purpose in my life, not to mention the fact that I was becoming increasingly aware of how I could now identify with so many of my clients who complained of the same way of life. This was disheartening, and I often wondered whether or not I would ever be able to achieve what I wanted.

But therein lays the problem. When it came down to it, and when I really thought about it, I realized that I actually didn't know what that was. I really didn't know what I wanted out of life, which also meant that I probably wasn't going to get it. So I, like so many other people on this planet, did in life, what I thought was expected of me, instead of finding my passion and living my life *on* purpose. And that was partly because I just didn't know what that *purpose* was. No wonder I was stuck.

I did however have a vision, kind of! I just didn't know how I was going to get it. I never made goals because I hated the thought of having to do so, and certainly didn't like to follow them. Or at least, that was what I thought.

However as I tried to figure out what my passions were, or what my purpose was supposed to be in life, and I thought about the things that had brought me satisfaction, fulfillment and contentment, I started to realize that they were in fact goals driven. I just had not thought of them that way.

So with this in mind I started to set goals in other areas of my life, but I was not getting the same success. The reason being was that the goals which I set and achieved on a daily basis had been what I now call unconscious goals. I say unconscious, because I was able to achieve them without really even considering them as goals, and I didn't really need think too much about them. They were goals that had become habits which I had unconsciously created formulas for achieving them. This is something that we all do every day without even thinking about it.

However, when it comes to setting new or bigger goals it can be a very different story. And since a lot of our goals will be new ideas, meaning that we will not have had the experience of achieving them in the past, then we probably wouldn't have any sort of formulae or pattern to follow until we reach the end. And this is something that we often need in order to make our goals easier to commit to, and ultimately achieve.

After realizing this, and taking a few goal setting workshops, I was still not able to follow through or achieve my goals so I found the whole process very frustrating. It seemed that there were often things that got in the way of my success. So, I started to look into what actually prevents people from achieving their goals and why do so many of us let ourselves down. And *why* do so few people actually ever follow through to achieve their New Year Resolutions. And I realized that a lot of the simplistic methods of goal setting do not necessarily address all of those nitty, gritty little details that have the power to either help or hinder our success.

Based on this awareness, and determined to find solutions to these problems I turned to methods such as NLP, mind/body therapies, visualizations and other little tricks, and created a formula which can be applied to any goal in hopes that it will help you achieve any of your goals. My purpose of writing this book, New Year Resolutions, Goals, Dreams and Aspirations is to help you both set great goals and to make it as simple as possible for you to follow through and ultimately achieve them too.

Suzanne is a Coach, Author and Facilitator who uses NLP, Thought Felid Therapy, Mind/Boyd Therapies, Myers Briggs Personality Profiling and Solution Focussed Coaching.

She also writes for The Singles Times, online dating magazine, and is the author of How To Turn That First Glance Into A Date. She has several other books, DVD projects and documentary projects in the works.

You can learn more about Suzanne and her upcoming projects, workshops and events by visiting her website www.suzanneprice.com This site will be updated frequently.

As A Coach

As a coach I can assist you to uncover your passions and purpose in life so that you can define the person who you truly want to be. I will listen to your dreams and encourage you to become the best version of yourself possible while motivating you to create the life you want to live.

As a coach I can assist you in finding clarity in your life and help you to create a very inspirational vision for success. I can help you develop crystal clear goals and an achievable plan of action, and help you to identify and utilize your best personal motivational strategies.

As a coach I can help you to identify any limiting or conflicting beliefs, obstacles, objections or self-sabotaging behaviours which get in your way of success, and then together we can work on strategies to abolish or overcome them.   I can also help you overcome your fears, and challenge you to identify all of the aspects of your life which are unsatisfactory.

As a coach I will motivate you to move forward while holding you accountable for your actions. I can inspire motivate and challenge you to succeed in all of your personal, professional and emotional goals, while encouraging you to create and maintain more balance in your life.

Some Areas That I Specialize In Coaching

Dating & Finding A Relationships

Meeting Mr. Right, Meeting Miss Right

How To Turn That First Glance Into A Date

How To Have A Successful Internet Date

How To Turn That First Date Into A Second

How To Turn That Date Into Happily Ever After

Meeting People & Making Friends

Overcoming The Fear Of Rejection

Overcoming Shyness & Social Phobias

Personal Style & Image Consulting

Communication & Social Skills

Building Confidence

Personal & Professional Development

Personal Success

Achieving Your Goals Dreams & New Year\s
Resolutions

Finding Clarity In Your Life

Finding Your Passion & Living Your Life With Purpose

Creating Balance In Your Life

Becoming The Person You Aspire To Be

Becoming Confident At Speaking Up In Public

Overcoming Stage Fright

Being Seen, Time To Step Into The Lime Light

Living Your Dream

Stress Management

Overcoming Your Fears

Creating A New Identity

Living Life With Style

Becoming The Best Version Of Yourself Possible.

www.ingramcontent.com/pod-product-compliance
Lightning Source LLC
Chambersburg PA
CBHW072126090426
42739CB00012B/3075